1511.3

DATE

MAR

cornerstone
LIVING LIBRARY
869 Cole Dr., Lilburn, GA 30047

LET'S VISIT SOUTH KOREA

Let's visit
SOUTH KOREA

PATRICIA SHEPHEARD

ACKNOWLEDGEMENTS

The Publishers are grateful to the following organizations and individuals for permission to reproduce copyright illustrations in this book:

> Dawn Farnham; Michael de Havilland; Ann Hills; Hutchison Photo Library; the Korea National Tourist Corporation; Korean National Museum; Overseas Missionary Fellowship; Popperfoto; Patricia Shepheard; South Korean Ministry of Culture and Information; TRIP; Zhang Shui Cheng.

© Patricia Shepheard 1988

All rights reserved. No reproduction, copy or transmission of this publication may be made without written permission.

No paragraph of this publication may be reproduced, copied or transmitted save with written permission or in accordance with the provisions of the Copyright Act 1956 (as amended), or under the terms of any licence permitting limited copying issued by the Copyright Licensing Agency, 7 Ridgmount Street, London WC1E 7AE.

Any person who does any unauthorized act in relation to this publication may be liable to criminal prosecution and civil claims for damages.

First published 1988

Published by MACMILLAN PUBLISHERS LTD
Houndmills, Basingstoke, Hampshire RG21 2XS
and London
Companies and representatives
throughout the world

Designed and produced by Burke Publishing Company Limited
Pegasus House, 116-120 Golden Lane
London EC1Y 0TL, England

Printed in Hong Kong

British Library Cataloguing in Publication Data
Shepheard, P.
Let's visit South Korea.—(Let's visit).
1. Korea (South)—Social life and customs—
Juvenile literature
I. Title
951.9'5043   DS922.27
ISBN 0-333-45696-3

AUTHOR'S NOTE

In spite of extensive travelling and reading, and the help and friendliness of many South Koreans, a year is a short visit for writing such a book. However, I have been lucky in receiving the advice of many people with much greater expertise than mine. In particular, I should like to thank the Royal Asiatic Society's Korea Branch; the Korea Insights programme of the YWCA; the Korea National Tourism Corporation; the Ministry of Culture and Information; Ms Sue Bae; Mrs Chong, Ern Hee, Mr Kim, Gwon Gu; Dr Jim Grayson and Dr Ruth Grayson; Dr Horace Underwood; Mr Dick Meakins; and my own family for all their help and support. Any shortcomings, of course, are entirely my own.

Contents

	Page
Map	6
Land of the Morning Calm	7
The Birth of Korea	18
The Recent Past	31
An Economic Miracle	39
A Melting Pot of Beliefs	48
East Meets West in South Korean Culture	58
Daily Life	68
The Countryside	82
Into the Twenty-first Century	90
Index	94

Land of the Morning Calm

A look at a map of Asia shows the Korean peninsula to be joined like a finger half way up the hand of the Far Eastern coast. It seems to be stretching out to reach the crescent of large islands which form Japan, as if trying to link them to the enormous land masses of China and the Soviet Union. Indeed, through the centuries, Korea has often acted as a link between Japan and the giants of mainland Asia. Most of the peninsula's northern border is with China, but 16 kilometres (10 miles) of it is with the Soviet Union. The shortest distance between South Korea and Japan is about 200 kilometres (124 miles).

For over a thousand years, the Korean peninsula with its accompanying three thousand islands was ruled as one country of about 220,000 square kilometres (85,000 square miles). Since 1945, the peninsula has been administered as two separate countries internationally known as South Korea (or the Republic of Korea) and North Korea (or the Democratic People's Republic of Korea). Although South Korea looks

Seagulls hover over the rocky shores of Hong Island. There are some three thousand islands around the Korean peninsula

small next to the enormous expanses of China, the Soviet Union and the Pacific Ocean, it covers an area of nearly 100,000 square kilometres (39,000 square miles)—about the same size as Iceland, New Zealand or Portugal. This is about forty-five per cent of the area of the whole Korean peninsula and islands. The population of South Korea is over forty million, compared to North Korea's nineteen million.

South Korea is on similar latitudes to Greece, southern Spain and California. However, its climate is much more extreme, with the lowest temperatures around minus 20 degrees Celsius (minus 4 degrees Fahrenheit) and the highest recorded temperature at 40 degrees Celsius (104 degrees Fahrenheit). This means that the winters can be very cold with plenty of snow, although the dryness of the air encourages the snow to evaporate, so it does not usually become very deep. The summers, on the other hand, are very hot and wet. Most of the rain falls in July and August, often during storms caused by violent winds known as typhoons. In Seoul, the capital, the average winter temperature is minus 5 degrees Celsius (23 degrees Fahrenheit) while the average summer temperature is 25 degrees Celsius (77 degrees Fahrenheit).

The weather is at its most pleasant during spring (from March to May) and autumn (from September to November). The autumn is usually chosen for big international gatherings like the International Monetary Fund meeting in 1985, the Asian Games in 1986 and the Olympic Games in 1988.

South Korea has extremes not only of climate, but also of terrain. Nearly seventy per cent of the land is covered with hills and mountains. With the highest peaks mainly in the north and the east, the mountains become lower and more scattered towards the southwest. The old, rugged mountains, mainly of granite and limestone, are not very high. They are popular with hikers and mountaineers.

Nowadays, the Korean peninsula is not volcanic or prone to earthquakes. However, the highest mountain in South Korea is an extinct volcano. This is Mount Halla (nearly 2,000 metres or 6,600 feet) on Cheju Island. Cheju is Korea's largest island and lies about 140 kilometres (87 miles) south of the peninsula.

One of the earlier names of Korea is *Choson*, meaning "land

Fresh snow in the courtyard of Kyongbok Palace in Seoul. The dryness of the air encourages the snow to evaporate, so it rarely becomes very deep

of the morning calm", and the early morning mists among the woods and peaks explain this beautiful name. Even in the big cities, many Koreans go up the mountains as early as five o'clock in the morning to collect the pure spring water, to do physical exercises, or to shout out their frustrations from an isolated peak in preparation for the hustle and bustle of the day.

Another remarkable feature of South Korea's geography is the large tidal range on the west coast. In the northwest of the country this can be as much as 9.3 metres (30 feet). By the time an unsuspecting holiday-maker has come back from a swim in the sea, his or her towel may well have been swept away by the tide! The most popular holiday beaches are therefore on the east coast, where the sea is also much cleaner.

Most of South Korea's people live in a diagonal strip running from northwest to southeast. This is where the best farming land is and where most of the good roads and railways have been built. The main cities are Seoul and Inchon in the northwest, Taegu which lies southeast of the centre and Pusan in the southeast. The south and west coasts are also more accessible for fishing.

Due to its wide range of climates and terrain, South Korea has a great variety of plants. Some flourish in warm weather,

The crater of Mount Halla, an extinct volcano and South Korea's highest mountain

East meets West in South Korea's capital city of Seoul. Kwangwhamun, one of the gates of ancient Seoul, is today surrounded by modern high-rise office blocks

like the camellias and peaches on the islands of Cheju and Ullung and along the south coast. Others are adapted to the cold, such as junipers, spruce and gentians which grow in the north and on high mountains. The many gorgeous flowering shrubs include rhododendrons, azaleas and a kind of hibiscus called "rose of Sharon", chosen as the national flower because of its toughness, beauty and long flowering season.

There are more than 158 types of tree native to Korea. Among them are pine and bamboo—considered to be symbols of long life, they are often depicted on ornaments and furniture. The most common fruits are apples, pears, peaches, persimmons, figs, plums, apricots, quinces and oranges. Nuts include walnuts, chestnuts and pine kernels. Gingko trees, whose brilliantly yellow leaves decorate many roads in the autumn, also bear edible fruit. The largest and oldest gingko tree in the East—61 metres (200 feet) tall and 4.5 metres (15 feet) in diameter—grows near a temple at Yongmun-sa, about 48 kilometres (30 miles) east of Seoul.

One of Korea's most famous plants is ginseng. This plant is now widely cultivated, although the wild mountain variety is the most sought after. Its roots, which are believed to give strength and health, are used in many foods, drinks and medicines.

South Korea's mountains, once thickly forested, had become almost bare by the first half of the twentieth century because of war and the demands for fuel and timber. There was such

Freshly picked persimmons, a delicious pulpy fruit popular in Southeast Asia

serious concern about the resulting soil erosion, as well as the shortage of forests, that a United Nations Organization (UN) report of 1969 feared the damage might have gone too far to be corrected. As a result, a vigorous ten-year plan was introduced in 1973 in which communities had to plant and tend their own trees, while restrictions were imposed on felling trees and gathering leaves. Spurred on by the slogan "Love trees, love your country", the aims of the plan—to plant 2,132 million saplings—were achieved in only six years and a new ten-year plan was launched. Forests now cover two-thirds of South Korea, with all but the most barren of mountains having a rich tree covering. However, South Korea still has to import eighty-five per cent of its timber.

Ginseng plants growing in a mountain forest. The wild variety is especially prized

Autumn colours on the slopes of Mount Sorak in the east. Young forests, like this one, have been planted during the government reforestation campaigns begun in 1973

Korea is home to a wide variety of animals and birds. More than 370 species of birds have been recorded there, of which about 270 are migrating. These stay on the peninsula for only a limited season. As a result of the widespread destruction of the forests and the killing of birds for food or sport, several species nearly disappeared and one, the stork, is no longer found in South Korea. There is now strict government control on the shooting of birds. In fact, twenty particularly endangered species, including the Tristram woodpecker and the Manchurian crane, have been named "living national treasures" and enjoy special protection. In the late 1970s, when it was thought that the Manchurian crane was more or less extinct in

The Demilitarized Zone, marking the frontier between the North and the South. Free from people and pollution, it has become a haven for endangered species of animals and plants

South Korea, a colony of the birds was found in the Demilitarized Zone between North and South Korea.

This strip of land, declared a Demilitarized Zone at the end of the Korean War in 1953, is almost free of people. It is just 4 kilometres (2.5 miles) wide and snakes across the peninsula for 243 kilometres (150 miles). Although it was established for political reasons, it has provided for several endangered species a haven from pollution and people. As well as the birds already mentioned, it shelters rare plants including white gentians, and some shy animals, such as the Korean wildcats and brown bears.

In the mountainous and more remote regions of South

Korea there are also wild mammals such as deer, roe deer, weasel, lynx, badger, shrew, marten, boar and the occasional bear, wolf or leopard. However, a more common sight is one of the many varieties of snake. These seem to have flourished in spite of being in great demand for soup and various medicines. (Only one variety is deadly poisonous.)

From 1972 until 1981 all hunting was banned—since then, some has been allowed between November and February, but in a different one of the nine provinces each year. Unfortunately, despite these controls, industrial pollution and the spreading network of roads and railways still act against the wildlife.

Attempting to balance these factors is one of the ways in which South Korea is trying to preserve its magnificent natural environment, while providing a healthier and more comfortable life for its growing population.

The Birth of Korea

Korean tales often begin "When tigers smoked..."—the equivalent of "Once upon a time". Tigers are important in Korean tradition. They are seen as creatures that are sometimes rather silly, but which must nonetheless be respected because of their strength. They are often shown on the gates of houses to protect the inhabitants from evil, and a young playful little tiger, called *hodori*, was chosen as the mascot for the 1988 Seoul Olympic Games.

The oldest Korean myth of all, concerning the origins of Korea itself, involves a tiger. It is said that Hwanung, the son of the Creator, came down with three thousand companions to rule the earth. He heard the prayers of a bear and a tiger, both of whom wanted to become human. He gave them each some garlic and mugwort to eat and told them to withdraw from the light of the sun for one hundred days. The animals ate the plants and retired to their caves. The tiger became restless, and came out into the sunshine. The bear remained inside and

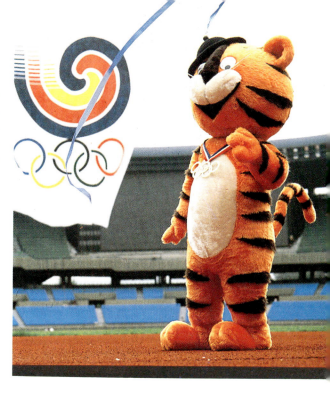

A playful little tiger called *hodori*. This was chosen as a mascot for the 1988 Olympic Games

passed the test. He was transformed into a beautiful woman and gave birth to Tangun, the founder of Korea (then called Choson) whose family reigned from 2333 BC to 1122 BC. The first capital of this kingdom was Pyongyang, now the capital city of North Korea. Tangun is said to have been wise and just, teaching the people to farm and to work happily together. Even today, people commemorate him and hold services at his altar on a mountain near Seoul on October 3, the national holiday of Foundation Day, also called Tangun Day.

The details of this story are unlikely, but it does contain some facts. It seems that the leading family of the first large political unit to emerge in Korea had a bear as their symbol and claimed that they were Tangun's descendants. The name given to their country is Ancient Choson and it lay between the Liao and Taedong rivers in the north of the peninsula.

Certainly, people were living and farming in the Korean peninsula at the time ascribed to Tangun. In fact, archaeological evidence suggests that people first lived in Korea more than four hundred thousand years ago. Then, about five thousand years ago, wandering tribes from North and Central Asia (called Altaic people) entered the Korean peninsula and found people already living there called Paleoasians. It is from the arrival of the Altaic people that Koreans date their five-thousand-year-old culture.

This comb-patterned jar found in Seoul is nearly five thousand years old, although archaeological evidence suggests that people first lived in the peninsula four hundred thousand years ago

The newcomers spoke a language related to Turkish, Hungarian and Finnish, which later adopted many Chinese words and, more recently, added some Japanese forms of speech to become modern Korean, spoken throughout North and South Korea. Gradually, as the people settled, they organized themselves into small tribal groups and developed farming, fishing and the accompanying civilization. The chiefs of friendly tribes used to meet to discuss matters of common interest, or any conflicts. A king was selected from among them and by the first century BC a council system of government was established, which later became known as *hwabaek*.

Throughout history, Korea has had strong links with China. Even during these very early days, there is evidence of common agricultural and manufacturing skills—in farming techniques, in the styles of pottery and in the making of silk. The Koreans also adopted the Chinese system of writing, involving thousands of separate characters, each denoting a whole word, although it was only the rich and highly educated who were able to learn to read with this complicated system. Having adopted China's writing system, the Koreans were strongly influenced by its literature and philosophy. However, they clung fiercely to their political independence, and although the Chinese often tried to absorb Korea into their own country, local resistance always forced them out within a few decades.

Two thousand years ago, there were three main kingdoms in

the Korean peninsula. They had absorbed most of the smaller kingdoms and each was hoping to expand further, which would mean moving into some of the territory of the other two kingdoms. As different kingdoms became stronger, the boundaries between them moved back and forth.

The largest of the kingdoms and the first to become well established, was Koguryo (37 BC—AD 688) in the north. Being close to China greatly helped Koguryo's development; its government used the newly invented Chinese official style of writing, while its scholars studied Chinese classics. In AD 372, Koguryo adopted Buddhism as its state religion. However, it paid the penalty of being close to China: the rulers of China wanted Koguryo to become part of their country and therefore attacked frequently.

The second of the three kingdoms was Paekche (18 BC—AD 660), in the southwest. The people here developed astronomy, medicine, geography, agriculture, metallurgy and music, taking so many of their ideas and works of art across the sea to Japan that the Japanese called Paekche "treasure land of gold and silver". Paekche adopted Buddhism about ten years after Koguryo and, in AD 552, introduced Buddhist images and teaching into Japan. In AD 475, Paekche's capital was taken over by Koguryo, and Paekche moved its new capital further south, first to a town now called Kongju, and then to one called Puyo. At both these places there are still many remains of this highly artistic kingdom—elaborate gold crowns, jade ornaments and bronze mirrors found in royal tombs there, and stone carvings from the Buddhist temples. Among the jade ornaments are the famous comma-shaped jewels.

Silla (57 BC—AD 668), in the southeast, was initially the smallest of the three kingdoms. It was also the last to adopt Buddhism as the religion of the royal family. It was famous for the development of *hwarang*, a voluntary social organization for boys from aristocratic families. They trained in the arts of war, studied literature together and learned to care for their neighbours. The five educational objectives were summarized as follows: loyalty to the monarch, respect for one's parents, being a reliable and warm friend, never giving up in war and avoiding unnecessary killing. To the *hwarang*, as to many later generations of Korean thinkers, truth was to be sought in a harmonious balance between traditional beliefs and new religions. As Silla became more powerful and its culture became more developed, it was happy to learn from its neighbours, borrowing ideas from Paekche and Koguryo, as well as sending monks to study in China.

Eventually, after much fighting and scheming, Silla came to rule most of the population of the former three kingdoms. This was the era sometimes called Korea's "golden age of art and culture". The Silla leaders built many beautiful temples and shrines and invented *idu*, a simpler system of writing Korean words using Chinese characters. They distributed land to the poor and built reservoirs to irrigate the rice fields.

The Silla capital was in southeast Korea, at the town now called Kyongju. Kyongju is one of the most popular historical

A fifth-century gold-and-jade crown of the Silla kings

sites and it is sometimes called "a museum without walls". Remains of palaces, temples and tombs reveal outstanding achievements in architecture, sculpture, painting, ceramics, jewellery, astronomy, medicine and literature.

Although at first they were very popular, by the early tenth century the Buddhist leaders had become too rich, greedy and lazy. They and members of the royal family were always fighting among themselves. Gradually, some of the local leaders and scholars broke away. One of them, Wang Kon, was eventually accepted as leader throughout the country. He became the founder and king of the new nation of Koryo. The name was a short form of Koguryo and is the origin of the modern word "Korea". Wang Kon (who became known after his death as *Taejo*, which means "Grand Ancestor") was a devout Buddhist. He built three hundred temples in his capital city of Kaegyong (now Kaesong in North Korea).

Koryo lasted from AD 918 to 1392. It had a very troubled existence. In the eleventh and twelfth centuries there were clashes with Chinese states demanding payment and obedience. Then, as in other parts of Asia and Europe, the Mongols kept invading. They did considerable damage throughout the kingdom and effectively ruled it for about a hundred years. They ensured that the Koryo princes married Mongol princesses and demanded large payments of gold, silver, horses,

Chomsongdae (which means "nearer-the-stars-place"), one of the oldest observatories in the world. It was built in AD 634 in Kyongju, the capital of the old Kingdom of Silla

ginseng, hawks for hunting, soldiers, workmen and women. They used the country as the base from which to attack Japan.

After the collapse of Mongol power in the fourteenth century, Koryo tried to reform its government by removing from power supporters of the Mongols and by trying to distribute more land to the poor. However, the reforms were resisted, as the people supposed to carry them out did not want to lose their own land. At the same time, Japanese pirates had become very well organized and were attacking not only at sea, but deep into Koryo as well. The situation did not improve until Yi Song-gye took over the leadership.

Like Wong Kon (the first king of Koryo), Yi became known as *Taejo* or "Grand Ancestor". He was dedicated to reforming the government, emphasizing many of the ideas of the Chinese philosopher Confucius. To do this, he closed some Buddhist temples and removed property from others which had become too rich and powerful. He replaced the Buddhist custom of cremating the dead by a form of burial, and he introduced ceremonies of ancestor remembrance which continue in Korea to this day.

The basic form of government set up by Yi and his descendants lasted for the next five hundred years and was known as the "Yi dynasty" or the "Choson dynasty". Their system of government gave most of the power and money to the senior officials and these positions were open only to the small group of nobles. There was endless scheming and competition among the nobles for the important jobs, in spite

Changdok Palace, a Yi dynasty palace in Seoul. It was originally built in 1405, it was then burnt down by the invading Japanese in 1592 and reconstructed in 1611

of the risk that such jobs were unlikely to last long and often ended in exile, punishment or even execution.

King Sejong, who reigned from 1418 to 1450, was widely thought to have been Korea's greatest ruler. He cared for his people and for his country and achieved outstanding developments in human knowledge. Firstly, he had the world's first pluviometer developed to measure rainfall (both for scientific purposes and to help the farmers). He encouraged research in sundials, clocks and astronomy.

He also restored the northern territory and regained Tsushima Island from the Japanese, while allowing them to continue trading there. In spite of the greedy aristocrats, King

Sejong actually managed to reform the taxation and rent systems.

However, his greatest feat was the invention of the Korean alphabet, called *hangul* (meaning "the great writing"). Up until that time, two other kinds of writing had been used, both very difficult to learn: the Indian Devangari script and Chinese characters. King Sejong wanted a phonetic system, in which each letter denotes a particular sound. *Hangul*, probably adapted from the Devangari script, involves twenty-nine simple letters. This remarkable system, launched in 1446, made it possible for almost everyone to learn to read and write, although Koreans continued to use Chinese characters for

A calligrapher at work. South Koreans are very proud of their alphabet

important documents. Even today, Chinese characters are usually mixed in with *hangul*. Koreans are so proud of their *hangul* alphabet that they have an annual national holiday to celebrate it.

Besides the internal difficulties of the Choson dynasty, there was also continuing trouble from outside the kingdom. In 1592, Japan invaded, making the royal family flee north to the Chinese border to ask the Chinese Ming dynasty for help. Meanwhile, a Korean admiral, Yi Sun-sin, had the brilliant idea of giving his ships the protection of iron armour—these became the world's first ironclad ships. The iron roofs over the decks made them look rather like turtles, so they were called "turtle ships". With these ships, Admiral Yi defeated the Japanese navy and cut off the supplies for the Japanese armies. This, combined with continual scattered fighting against the Japanese and the arrival of the Chinese forces, persuaded the Japanese to negotiate for peace.

The Japanese invasions, combined with attacks by the Manchus (from Manchuria, in what is now northeast China), caused terrible devastation. During the next two to three hundred years, the country became known as the Hermit Kingdom due to its understandable reluctance to admit outsiders. However, the invasions continued. Attracted by Korea's geographical position, its people and its good agriculture and minerals, foreigners would not leave it alone. Towards the end of the nineteenth century, both France and the United States of America attacked, though unsuccessfully.

A statue of Admiral Yi, a national hero who repelled the Japanese navy in the late sixteenth century with his fleet of the world's first ironclad ships

Troops were sent in by Japan, China and Russia, and in 1885 Great Britain occupied the island of Komundo for nearly two years until the Russians withdrew their demands to have Korea as their protectorate.

The Hermit Kingdom was reluctantly dragged out of its isolation. From 1882 onwards, it signed treaties of friendship and cooperation with the USA, Great Britain, Germany, Austria, Russia, Italy and France. However, local rebellions caused by government policies and enormous taxes gave foreign countries continual excuses to bring in troops. In this way, they were able to apply pressure on the Choson government, until eventually Japan took control, having defeated China in 1895 and Russia in 1905.

The Recent Past

In 1905, Japan proclaimed military control over Korea, which was to last until the end of the Second World War in 1945. Korea hoped that other countries such as the USA or Great Britain would object. However, they remained silent, recognizing Japan's political, military and economic interests in Korea and accepting its claim that the Koreans were probably too backward to run an efficient, modern government themselves.

The following year, in spite of the fact that the Korean Prime Minister refused to sign, the Japanese managed to get five Korean ministers to sign a treaty making Korea a Japanese protectorate. The Japanese increased their control of Korea until, in 1907, King Kojong tried to get international support for Korea's freedom. He received a sympathetic response, but no offers of help. The Japanese were so angry with him for complaining that they deposed him and made his son, Sunjong, king instead.

The next few years saw many major uprisings, riots, suicides and assassination attempts by Koreans in protest at the Japanese treaties, as well as many pleas to the USA and Great Britain for help. In 1909, a young Korean called An Chung-gun assassinated the Japanese Resident-General. Although he is now a national hero, his act was to no avail. In 1910, Korea formally became part of Japan.

The Japanese government helped its own citizens take over much of the business and land in Korea, with the result that most of the profits and nearly half the rice produced went to Japan. Japanese companies took control of most of the fisheries and allowed the felling of many of the trees. There was an attempt to bring all schools under government control. The Japanese language was to be used in schools and all public places; Korean history was not to be taught; Koreans had to adopt Japanese names and to take part in Japanese religious ceremonies.

However, the Japanese also modernized Korea. They built good roads, railways and ports, as well as dams to control the rivers and generate electricity. They developed many industries, particularly in the northern part of the country.

Many Koreans overseas were determined that their country should regain its independence and that they should have educated people ready for that time. For instance, in Manchuria in 1919 there were about 130 Korean schools and a Korean Independence Army was formed.

Other movements began in Korea itself. In 1919, King Kojong died. Soon after, the leaders of all the main religious groups planned a peaceful demonstration to appeal for independence. The main event was to be in the capital, Seoul, but similar events were planned throughout the country. This movement—called *Samil* ("March 1" in Korean)—was timed to coincide with the Paris Peace Conference after the First World War. The Japanese were furious and reacted violently, causing riots and reprisals all over the country. Over seven thousand Koreans are thought to have been killed at this time.

During the Second World War (1939-45) hundreds of thousands of Koreans were conscripted to work for the Japanese. However, the war ended with a victory for the Allies—the USA and the Soviet Union among them—and Japan was defeated. The USA and the Soviet Union each did not want the other to control the whole peninsula, so it was agreed that the Russians would accept the Japanese surrender north of the thirty-eighth parallel (38 degrees North line of latitude), while the Americans would accept it south of that line.

In 1948 the American troops left the southern territory, after elections sponsored by the United Nations Organization brought President Syngman Rhee to power. In the North, where the United Nations commission was refused entry, the Soviet-backed Prime Minister Kim Il Sung came to rule what had now become a separate country.

Once the Soviet and American troops had withdrawn from the two newly-independent Koreas, the North decided to try to reunite the country under its own government. In June 1950 the North Korean army crossed the thirty-eighth parallel, which had become the frontier between the two countries, driving the small and badly organized South Korean army down to the southernmost area around Pusan. The USA decided to intervene, with support from the United Nations, who sent some of the armed forces from sixteen other countries to their aid.

After a successful landing at Inchon, United Nations troops under the command of General Douglas MacArthur pushed back the North Korean army, advancing well beyond the thirty-eighth parallel. When they reached the Yalu River, which forms a natural frontier between North Korea and

The South Korean president Syngman Rhee *(right)* **and the American general Douglas MacArthur during the proclamation of the Republic of Korea in 1948. In his speech, MacArthur called for the barrier between the North and the South to be torn down**

China, the Chinese joined forces with the North Koreans, driving the United Nations troops back to the south.

When the Chinese entered the war in 1951 it became clear that neither side could hope to win quickly and that negotiations were a necessary step. These continued for two long years, as both Kim Il Sung on the one hand and General MacArthur and President Rhee on the other wanted to reunite the two Koreas on their own terms. In the meantime, the casualties among soldiers and civilians were mounting: there were about one million dead and wounded on the United Nations/South Korean side, while the combined Chinese and North Korean casualties reached an estimated one million and a half.

Peace talks were disrupted by disagreements within the South Korean side. Part of the UN command objected to General MacArthur's battle plan of pushing back beyond the thirty-eighth parallel for fear that they would be accused of aggression, while President Rhee supported the General. Finally, in spite of the South Korean objections, an armistice (cease-fire) was signed in July 1953. Following its terms, there is now a Demilitarized Zone (DMZ) some 4 kilometres (2.5 miles) wide, separating the two Koreas around the thirty-eighth parallel. There are also about forty thousand American troops stationed in South Korea with the agreement of the South Korean government,

A military Armistice Commission (MAC) ensures that the terms of the armistice agreement are kept. The Commission,

During the Korean War orphaned children like these carried their belongings and their younger siblings to unknown, but hopefully safer, destinations

which meets at the truce town of Punmunjom in the DMZ, consists of ten senior officers—five representing the South Korean/United Nations side and five from the North Korean/Chinese side.

Thus, the old kingdom of Choson has now become two countries. North Korea has taken the official name of the Democratic People's Republic of Korea, while its people continue to call it Choson. Its government is strongly influenced by China and the Soviet Union. South Korea is in turn influenced by the USA. Its official name is the Republic of Korea, although its people call it *Hanguk,* an abbreviation of *Taehan Minguk,* meaning "the nation of the great Han people".

The presidency of Syngman Rhee (1948-60), marked by corruption and riots, ended with Rhee's resignation. During the rule of President Park Chung Hee, who came to power after the 1961 military coup, a new constitution was drawn up which did away with direct elections of the country's president. Instead, the president was to be chosen by a group of people called an electoral college, who would themselves be elected by the general public. This angered a great many South Koreans, who felt that their country had become undemocratic. Their protests often ended in confrontations with the army and the police. The most violent incident took place in 1980 in Kwangju, where several hundred people were killed.

Widespread protests, calling for changes in the constitution to provide for proper elections and allow opposition parties to operate, continued during the presidency of Chun Doo Hwan, a retired general who had taken control of the country in 1980. In 1987, Chun postponed once again the long-awaited public debate on constitutional reforms. This, police brutality, suspected corruption and Chun's decision to appoint a former general—Roh Tae Woo—as the only presidential candidate of the ruling party, led to a wave of unrest in the country. In May 1987, various factions of the opposition united to form the National Council for Democratic Constitution. Buddhist and Confucianist organizations, as well as the Christian churches, appealed for a peaceful transition to a more democratic public life.

Various concessions were made—not only as a result of the internal protest but also in response to pressure from the outside world and with an eye on the Olympic Games scheduled to be held in Seoul in 1988.

In less than forty years, South Korea has experienced five different constitutions, three periods of martial law (military rule) and several outbreaks of riots and demonstrations claiming many lives. The country is still searching for the best form of democratic government to continue its prosperous development and defend its security, while allowing more freedom and responsibility to its individual citizens.

An Economic Miracle

In the early 1960s, South Korea was one of the poorest countries in the world and many people had no jobs. Some of the reasons for this were connected with the country's geography and natural resources. Its territory is small in proportion to its population and most of the land is covered with steep hills or rocky mountains, leaving only about one-fifth for cultivation. It has a temperate climate with very cold winters, so usually only one rice crop can be grown each year. It is short of minerals and has to import nearly all its raw materials and energy.

There were also historical reasons for the poverty. The Hermit Kingdom's policies had not emphasized science, trade and industry, so the country had fallen behind in these fields. Under the Japanese occupation, nearly all the power stations together with the heavy and chemical industries were developed in the northern half of the peninsula, now North Korea, while most of the farmland and fishing areas had been overworked and spoilt. There was a shortage of skilled people and leaders because, during the occupation, the Japanese had themselves held most of the technical, engineering and senior management jobs. Education for Koreans had been so limited that many had not even learned to read. The Korean War caused further havoc. Half the manufacturing facilities, nearly half the homes, a quarter of the schools and much land and other facilities were destroyed. The people felt lost and hopeless.

The political situation introduced further problems. The country was even more crowded than before, because many Koreans came to the South from North Korea, as well as from China and Japan. Korea had always acted as a bridge between China and Japan, but South Korea could no longer trade in this way because of its sealed border with North Korea and hostile relations with China. The fear that North Korea might attack again meant that nearly one-third of government spending had to go on defence.

It is remarkable that, with all these disadvantages, South Korea has had one of the fastest-growing economies in the world since the mid-sixties. It is the fourteenth largest trading nation in the world, the fourth largest exporter of footwear and the second largest shipbuilder. It has the world's largest cement plant and bone china factory.

This dramatic change was started under President Park's government, whose main aim was economic progress. The government began by reforming Korean currency—the *won*—

A dock at Inchon port. South Korea is the world's second largest shipbuilder (after Japan)

to encourage exports, by altering the banking system to make it easier for industrialists to borrow money, and by making careful five-year plans. For three years, people could see no progress. In fact, bad harvests resulted in such widespread hunger that there were strong protests against the government. However, at the same time, roads, schools, new factories and other necessary facilities were being built, so preparations were being made for economic development.

The first government plans aimed to establish a self-reliant economy, stressing the importance of agriculture and the building of the necessary roads, dams, ports, houses, factories and offices. Industries which produced items essential for other sectors, such as cement and fertilizers, were given priority in government aid. They then tried to modernize the economy, introducing light industries such as textiles and soft toys. This stage was followed by the introduction of electronics industries making simple radios and other unsophisticated pieces of equipment, as well as electronic components, such as small parts for televisions and washing machines. All these types of industries employed large numbers of people, but the equipment involved was neither expensive nor complicated. At that time, the workers' wages were low, so the companies could sell their products cheaply overseas. The next stage (in 1972-1976) was the introduction of heavy and chemical industries. These required very expensive equipment and complicated production techniques. They were usually established in

A display of soft toys in a Seoul market. Clothes and toys produced by South Korea's light industry are also sold abroad, bringing in large profits

The industrial complex at Pohang, one of the country's largest manufacturing centres producing iron and steel

cooperation with foreign companies and involved borrowing large amounts of money from abroad, as well as learning the necessary technology.

These early light and heavy industries continue. However, Korean firms have realized they can no longer rely on adopting and adapting ideas from other countries. The sixth five-year plan (1987-1991) emphasizes Korean investment in its own research and development.

If one idea is not working well, it is changed; successful ones are expanded. This approach of looking at each case carefully and quickly adapting the policies is an important feature of

Korea's success. It involves very firm, and sometimes unpopular, government action. Another aspect of the government's flexibility has been its use of money for public works. When the economy is doing well, government projects tend to be delayed to allow private companies to expand. However, when the economy is doing badly, the government boosts its programmes—such as building roads and houses—to make more jobs and to increase the demand for industrial products, like machinery and cement.

Sometimes new industries have been started by the government itself; sometimes it encouraged private businessmen to take the risk; and sometimes the two worked together. This involved close cooperation between the government and key businessmen, leading to some enormous business groups (called *chaebol* in Korean), each of which has a wide variety of interests. For example, one—Lucky-Goldstar—has twenty-four companies involved in chemicals, electronics, communications, oil refining, mining, construction, engineering, financial services, trade, distribution, education and other public services. The top thirty *chaebol* account for most of the country's exports and about one-third of all its economic activity. However, they are often not as profitable as smaller firms, sometimes because they have borrowed large amounts of money to start ambitious enterprises and are now having to pay for this.

The borrowing of money is inevitable in order to achieve an industrial expansion like South Korea's, but it does bring problems. South Korea was once the world's fourth largest debtor nation and, consequently, it has to pay a large proportion of its earnings to the banks from which it has borrowed. Up until 1985, the country imported more than it exported, so the debt kept increasing. However, in 1986, the situation was at last reversed.

The attempt to reduce the national debt takes two forms. The first is "import substitution". This means encouraging local industries to make items that are being imported. This has included many daily necessities such as clothes, crockery, kitchen utensils, domestic appliances and simple farm equipment. The second attack on the national debt comes from encouraging exports. Having started by exporting articles dependent on its supply of cheap labour, such as clothing and electronic components, South Korea has adapted to the rising price of its labour by increasing the sophistication of its exports. For instance, electronic items provide about one-seventh of the exports. Whereas they used to be made mostly with fairly simple equipment but intensive labour, more and more factories are now highly automated and products like computers, video-tape recorders, car components and semi-conductors are increasing.

As a result of its lack of natural resources, including oil, South Korea is closely affected by changes in world trade. Its main overseas customer is the USA, so it depends on a sustained American demand for its products. South Korea has many companies working in overseas construction which

A view of the Seoul–Pusan expressway which links South Korea's major cities and runs from the northwest to southeast

depend on foreign countries needing and being able to afford large building projects. They suffer when there is unrest in those countries.

There are many illustrations of South Korea's dramatic progress. In 1961 there were 25,000 kilometres (16,000 miles) of paved roads. Today there are well over 50,000 kilometres (31,000 miles). These include a 420-kilometre (260-mile) motorway from Seoul to Pusan that many said was too difficult to build. (It was, in fact, built at one-seventh of the cost per kilometre of a comparable road in Japan, but at considerable human cost as many workmen died in the rush to build quickly and cheaply.) Another illustration are the bridges on the River Han in Seoul. In 1950, it had just one bridge which was then destroyed in the Korean War. Today there are eighteen, as well as extensive riverside parks, flood barriers and motorways.

South Korea has shown such a great ability to cope successfully with its own economic changes since the early 1960s that some have called it "an economic miracle". Of course, the so-called miracle has been created by the Koreans themselves. It has involved several ingredients: a determined government, hard-working and low-paid people and adventurous business leaders.

A Melting Pot of Beliefs

According to tradition in Korea, the main blessings are seen as longevity (a long life), happiness, health, wealth and children. South Koreans have adopted a wide variety of beliefs in their search for these blessings.

As in many countries, the oldest religion is shamanism. This is belief in an invisible world of spirits existing alongside the world we can see. Sometimes the spirits interfere in the lives of humans and then people need a religious leader capable of going into a trance, who can act as a link between the spiritual world and the visible world; such a religious leader is called a shaman. This religion has existed in Korea for well over 2,500 years, having originally entered the country from Siberia.

The Korean shaman is usually a woman called a *mudang* and a ceremony in which she communicates with spirits is called a *kut*. Apart from her important job of contacting the spirits to discourage evil and obtain blessings, a *mudang* also has other roles. She is thought to cure diseases and personal problems.

A Korean shaman (priestess) called a *mudang* performs a dance which puts her in touch with spirits

Sometimes she foretells the future and gives advice, such as helping to choose a suitable husband or wife, a good day for a special event, or a place for burial which will be pleasing to the spirits. She may also provide entertainment with dancing and music.

The long traditions of shamanistic belief have had a deep effect on Korean life and thought. It is mainly the less educated and country people for whom shamanism is their

A man in traditional white mourning clothes

principal belief, although all Koreans are influenced by it in their customs and culture. Aspects of shamanism have also been absorbed into their other religions.

The first formalized, international philosophy of life to be accepted in Korea was Confucianism. This is based on the teaching of the Chinese philosopher Kung (known as Confucius) who lived twenty-five centuries ago. He emphasized the importance of study to discover the truth, and also of self-control, especially in human relationships. Confucius named five types of relationship with their key features. These are justice between ruler and subject, affection between father and son, prudence between husband and wife, order between old and young, and loyalty between friends. Koreans are very conscious of the appropriate behaviour and respect between people. This is reflected in their language, in which the form of the words chosen shows the relationship between speaker and listener, as well as the degree of respect for the subject of their conversation.

Certain Confucian customs are still widely practised in South Korea, including annual memorial ceremonies to family ancestors, mainly in the male line. However, since the 1890s the philosophy is no longer central to national life. In the past, examinations in the teaching of Confucius and his followers had been part of the selection for all important government

An ancient Confucian symbol of completeness, called *sam taeguk*. It is a common ornamental motif, found on doors, fans and shutters

jobs, and Confucianism had been the official state philosophy throughout the Choson dynasty (1392—1910). Now there are about two hundred and fifty meeting places and about eight hundred thousand Confucianists.

Only a small number of people who embrace Confucian values and practise Confucian principles consider themselves to be adherents of Confucianism as a religion. The majority of people offer sacrifices before ancestral tablets or graves only as a matter of custom, with few religious undertones.

With Confucianism, Korea absorbed the other great, ancient Chinese philosophy, Taoism (or "The Way"). This taught that happiness came from following the way of nature, the way of heaven and the way of earth. The symbols of its ideas are a common part of Korean life and include the *taeguk* in the centre of the national flag, four of the eight trigrams in the flag's corners and the *sam taeguk*—like the *taeguk,* only divided into three equal parts in blue, red and yellow and found on many fans and doors. The *Tao Te Ching* (The Book of The Way) is opposed to too much government, so its influence is more subtle than that of Confucianism with its many rules and ceremonies.

One of the most popular religions in South Korea is Buddhism, with about eight million followers and over seven thousand temples. This religion is based on the teachings of Siddhartha Gautama Sakyamuni (the Buddha), prince of a small kingdom on the borders of what are now India and Nepal, who lived in the sixth century BC. He taught that

A monk sounds the bell in a Buddhist temple. Bronze bells found at Buddhist shrines are often richly decorated

personal salvation came from renouncing worldly desires and being moderate in all things. This means that the perfect way of living can be discovered only by someone who is freed from hate and love and who is totally truthful.

Buddhists believe in reincarnation—a soul being reborn in a new body after death. They also believe that those who have learned to control their desires can escape the cycle of birth, growing old, sickness and death. This state of detachment is called "enlightenment" and anyone who achieves it can become a *buddha*. However, some enlightened people choose to continue being reborn, in order to help other people reach enlightenment; these are called *bodhisattvas*.

In the early centuries, Buddhism divided into two main

types. The one that came to Korea was the *mahayana* school, which preached that almost any method of reaching salvation is acceptable. This has meant that a wide range of customs have been adopted by Buddhists in Korea. There are eighteen main sects (forming The Council of Korean Buddhist Orders), as well as many minor sects. Most sects include sections which concentrate on Zen Buddhism (called *Son* in Korean), which emphasizes the value of meditation, or deep thought. Some sects (such as the Taego, Korea's second largest sect) allow their monks to marry. The nuns, who live in separate temples, are always unmarried, and they include many great teachers and leaders.

All the Buddhist sects have adopted some popular aspects of shamanism, such as worshipping the mountain spirit (shown as an old man with a friendly-looking tiger) and the seven-star spirit (based on the star constellation known as the Great Bear or the Plough). They see these as a way of encouraging people to come to the temple where they will then study the more central teachings of Buddhism.

Having been the state religion for nearly a thousand years of Korea's past, Buddhism has had a profound influence on its history and culture. This is acknowledged officially by the celebration of Buddha's birthday (usually in May) as a public holiday. It is marked by lectures, lantern parades, meditation sessions, dancing and concerts.

Christianity is the fastest-growing religion in South Korea today. The first known converts were some Koreans who went

Street celebrations of the Buddha's Birthday. Each lantern bears a tag on which people write names and addresses of their loved ones, to commend them to the Buddha

to Peking (Beijing) in 1784. There, they met Roman Catholic missionaries and were baptized. The first Catholic missionaries to Korea were Chinese in the 1790s and then French from the 1830s onwards. The first Protestant missionaries, Presbyterian and Methodist, arrived in 1885.

Christianity was started about two thousand years ago by Jesus Christ, a poor carpenter's son, in what is now Israel. He taught the importance of love, first of God, then of all people. The Christian message is to treat all people equally. It helps to give hope to the poor and the suffering.

Today there are about eight million Christians in Korea (over one million Roman Catholics and more than six million

The faithful on their way to a service in a popular evangelical church in Seoul. Christian religions have gained a large following in South Korea in recent years

Protestants), including some of the largest individual church memberships in the world. Some of the denominations have absorbed aspects of shamanism—these are apparent at revival meetings which are rather like a *kut,* and at centres which concentrate on curing diseases. Christianity has a strong influence as many of the country's leaders belong to one of the Christian churches.

Several smaller religious groups flourish in South Korea. *Taejonggyo*—teaching of the "Great Ancestor", and said to be about four thousand years old—is a form of shamanism based on the story of Tangun who was father, teacher and king of the Korean people from 2333 BC. Another religion unique to Korea is *Chondogyo* (originally called "Eastern learning"), which teaches that heaven and man are indivisible and all men are equal. It resisted foreign religions entering Korea and wanted to encourage Koreans' pride in their own country and traditions. It now has about fifty thousand followers.

Islam is the teaching of Muhammad who lived 11,400 years ago in what is now Saudi Arabia. His teachings entered Korea with some Turkish soldiers during the Korean War (1950-53). There are now more than thirty thousand Muslims (as Muhammad's followers are called) in Korea, with three temples (known as mosques).

While following one of these many religions, a Korean does not necessarily deny the others. For instance, he or she may choose a Christian wedding, perform annual Confucian ceremonies for the family's ancestors, visit a Buddhist temple to gain inner peace, and ask a *mudang* to bless a new house. Each religion may offer a glimpse of the truth, so it is socially acceptable to follow many, or none.

East Meets West in South Korean Culture

The Koreans are highly artistic people. They also love music, sport and parties. These tastes are reflected in their many festivals which feature singing, dancing, the arts and a variety of sports. The festivals are also a time for parties and for renewing loyalties to family and nation.

The year starts with a festival, New Year's Day. Like most people in the Orient, Koreans traditionally follow the lunar calendar, in which the year is divided into months of about twenty-nine days, corresponding to the cycles of the moon; each month starts with the new moon. The resulting year normally has twelve months, but to keep it in step with the seasons, an extra month is included every few years. The lunar New Year is in January or February of the solar (Western) calendar. Today, the Koreans celebrate both New Years—the Eastern and the Western—with parties, presents, new clothes and family visits.

Other national holidays centre round the family. One of the

Children flying kites on New Year's Day

greatest national festivals, *Chusok*, or the Harvest Moon Festival Day, is devoted to the remembrance of the dead, with families visiting the graves of their ancestors and viewing the full moon at night. Other national holidays celebrate the living; on Children's Day in May families concentrate on the younger generation. On that day children are often allowed free entrance to zoos, parks and funfairs.

Several holidays commemorate important national events, such as the launching of the Korean alphabet—*hangul*—in October 1446, the Japanese surrender in August 1945 and the proclamation of the Republic of Korea in July 1948. Two other holidays concentrate on key aspects of national life: Arbor Day on April 5 is a day for planting trees and remembering the importance of the environment; Armed Forces Day on October 1 is a day of military parades and ceremonies.

There are two national holidays which reflect Korea's two main religions—one Eastern and one Western. The Buddha's Birthday is on the eighth day of the fourth lunar month (usually in May) and is often called "The Feast of the Lanterns" because of the many lantern decorations in streets, temples and homes. Christmas, on December 25, is celebrated with church services, greeting cards, coloured lights and Christmas trees.

These national holidays and other festivals are often times for sports. The traditional sports of Korea include *taekwondo*,

Traditional Korean wrestling called *ssirum*. The aim of each wrestler is to get any part of the opponent's body other than his feet to touch the ground

A game of football, one of South Korea's most popular sports, at a Seoul stadium

ssirum, *yudo* and archery. *Taekwondo* is a self-defence martial art which began in Korea over two thousand years ago and is now popular in many countries. Its name means "hand and foot fighting" and it involves a variety of high kicks and strong arm gestures. *Ssirum* is a kind of wrestling, an ancient Korean sport which is still popular today. The rules are simple, the aim being to get any part of the opponent's body (other than the feet) to touch the ground. However, the techniques can be subtle and skilful. *Yudo* is a Korean sport similar to the Japanese judo, but older. Traditional Korean archery uses a bow which is smaller but more powerful than the usual international bow and it is a skill at which Koreans excel.

Since the end of the last century, internationally popular sports have gradually been introduced into Korea. Football,

A traditional masked dance. These are especially popular in the countryside

which came in 1882, is now probably the most popular sport in the country. A great boost was given to international sports in 1981 when Seoul was chosen to host the 1986 Asian Games and the 1988 Olympic Games. Enthusiasm for sports flourished and superb facilities were built or improved in the Seoul area, as well as in Taejon, Kwangju, Taegu and Pusan.

Music is an important part of Korean life. It is performed to accompany ceremonies, banquets and religious services, as well as work and pleasure. Most Koreans sing and dance, while many play musical instruments, often to internationally famous standards. In traditional Korean dances, men and women perform separately. There are several different types of dance, including a heritage of court, folk and religious dances. These are still popular, as are Western traditional ballet, modern ballet and disco.

The oldest music played in Korea is probably that performed twice a year at the Confucian shrine in Seoul. In the fifteenth century, King Sejong asked his assistants to work out how the ancient Chinese music must have sounded and it is the results of their research that are being played today. Although neglected during the period of westernization of Korea earlier this century, these types of Eastern classical music are now being revived and studied at many schools. Other schools concentrate on the rich heritage of Korean folk, shamanist and Buddhist music, or on Western classical music. Much to the surprise of many visitors to Korea, famous Western classical

A member of *Taechwita*, a traditional military band, playing a tune on a large shell. Despite competition from Western music, both classical and popular, ancient Korean music has a wide appeal

tunes are played everywhere—by doorbells, telephone systems and in dental surgeries and elevators.

As in sports and music, China was also the main external influence in fine arts until the twentieth century. Chinese art is full of symbolism and references to well-known legends, much of which has been adopted by the Koreans. Since the greatest blessing is thought to be long life, the ten Taoist symbols for long life are very common in Korean art. These are sun, moon (or deer), clouds, water, rocks, bamboo, pine trees, turtles, cranes and a mythical kind of mushroom called *pullocho*.

Ancient symbols adorn South Korea's national flag, adopted by the old Kingdom of Choson in 1882 and known as *Taegukki*. The centre part, called *taeguk*, shows the red and blue sections of the circle locked together harmoniously. They symbolize the existence of opposites in life—such as between male and female, or night and day—and their ultimate balance and harmony. In the corners of the white background there are four sets of three lines broken in different ways. These represent heaven, earth, fire and water—the four elements of the universe.

The Taoist twelve directional signs are also very popular. They correspond to twelve years in the Eastern calendar cycle and are: rat (or mouse), ox, tiger, rabbit, dragon, snake, horse, sheep (or goat), monkey, chicken, dog and pig (or hog). People are thought to take on some of the characteristics of the animal in whose year they are born and many take care to choose a suitable "animal" as a marriage partner. For example, 1972,

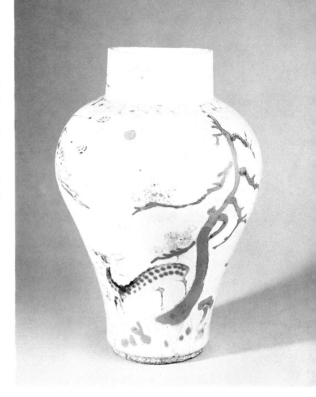

This nineteenth-century porcelain jar is decorated with most of the symbols of long life: sun, moon, deer, clouds, crane, mushroom and pine tree

1984 and 1996 are years at the beginning of a new cycle and so are years of the rat.

On walls, cloth, pottery and almost any other decorated surfaces, there are often what look like ornamental squiggles. These are usually stylized versions of Chinese characters for long life, joy, happiness, wealth and various other blessings. There are also ornate decorations on temples, which possess profound and detailed significance as well as beauty.

While following other traditions, particularly the Chinese, Korean artists have held on to their strongly independent national character. They are inclined to scorn technical

The South Korean flag, known as *Taegukki*. The paisley-shaped parts of the inner circle represent the reconciliation of opposites

perfection. For example, they do not like pottery that is perfectly symmetrical, but find a slightly uneven shape more beautiful and lifelike. Similarly, a traditional Korean roof has almost no straight lines—even the ridge is curved. Korean artists have tended to create works which look simple and natural, in contrast to the grander Chinese and more meticulous and elaborate Japanese styles. However, the Koreans have shown great technical skill, as in the famous Silla jewellery and Koryo celadons.

The Silla crowns and royal belts of the fifth and sixth centuries were magnificent creations of gold and jade. Again, the ornaments are rich in symbolism: the hundreds of decorative comma shapes might signify the moon (of great importance to a nomadic society), an unborn baby (stressing the value of new life), or tigers' claws (thought to destroy evil and help people have many children).

The Koryo celadons are pieces of pale greeny-blue pottery, of which the best were made between AD1150 and 1300. Some are plain and simple, while others are ornately decorated with symbols, such as those for long life. Today, almost every museum in the world has a treasured piece of such pottery, but the precise secret of the dyes and glazes used has been lost.

Nowadays, Korean artists continue to create all kinds of works of art, which express their talents and their love of nature, as well as the rich heritage of Korean culture.

An ornate Koryo celadon vase. The secret of making the inimitable pale green dye and glaze, which distinguish this pottery from any other, has been lost

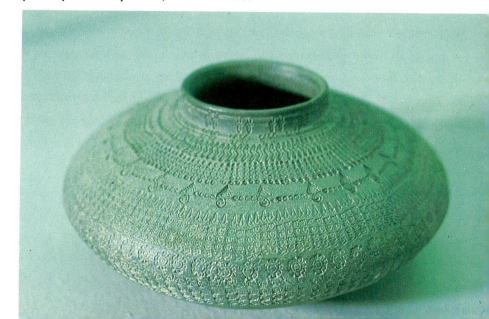

Daily Life

Life is changing fast in South Korea which, in twenty-five years, has developed from a poor farming society into a modern manufacturing and trading nation. Of course, this has brought many changes to people's daily life. Most people now live in towns and cities, with about one-quarter of the population living in the capital city of Seoul and another quarter in the four metropolitan areas of Pusan, Taegu, Inchon and Kwangju. These are all very large cities; Seoul, with over ten million people, is the fourth largest city in the world.

Many people moved to the towns and cities as refugees after the Korean War and during the rapid economic expansion of the last twenty years. As a result, there has been an enormous need for more housing. In the past, most Koreans lived in small, L-shaped, thatched houses, each in its own compound, often containing three or four generations of one family. Today, many of the townspeople live in massive appartment blocks, usually of twelve to twenty storeys. The average size of

A sixty-three storey Seoul skyscraper, once Asia's tallest building

a housing unit is small: about 74 square metres (790 square feet)—roughly the size of a badminton court. Although still small, these apartments do have the advantages of more modern facilities in water supply, electricity, sanitation and rubbish disposal.

The Koreans are used to crowded living conditions and thus their houses are usually without much furniture. People sleep on a special mattress, called a *yo*, which is rolled up during the daytime. Seating is usually on cushions on the floor, and meals are eaten off low tables, using chopsticks and spoons. The main furniture consists of chests of various sizes—for clothes,

69

The coalman has arrived with the household's supply of coal. South Korean houses are heated by underfloor pipes

books, bedding and cushions—many of which are very old and highly valued. Screens are popular as decoration and room dividers. Because they live so close to the floor, Koreans always take off their shoes when entering a home and take care to keep their floors very clean. They usually heat their homes by pipes under the floor, so the place of honour in the winter—usually given to the eldest person—is the warmest patch of the floor.

Another traditional feature of Korean homes are the *kimchi* pots. These are large earthenware pots, which used to be stored in a sunny corner of the courtyard, but are now often seen on roofs or verandahs. They contain *kimchi,* the pickled vegetables which are an important part of the Korean diet. The winter supply is made in the autumn when mountains of Chinese cabbage and white radishes are prepared and mixed with garlic, red pepper, salt and other vegetables and spices. While most Koreans eat some *kimchi* every day, the main ingredient of their diet is rice. In the past, when meat was a rare luxury, people depended on a variety of vegetables and fish, often dried to preserve it. However, the meat consumption is now increasing, pork being the most common. *Bulgogi* (barbecued beef) and *kalbi* (barbecued short ribs), both

Earthenware pots on sale in a Pusan street. They are used to store *kimchi*, a national staple of pickled cabbage and radishes

Dried saltfish at a Seoul market. Various types of dried fish are a common ingredient of many Korean dishes

prepared with ginger, garlic and spring onions, are among the most popular meat dishes. Koreans do not normally eat dessert, but end their meals with fruit, such as strawberries or pears. For special occasions, they make colourful little cakes of sweetened rice.

Most Koreans now wear Western clothes. South Korea produces clothes and shoes for export all over the world and thus has a wide and fashionable choice. The Japanese imposition of rather military school uniforms was discontinued a few years ago, but some schools have reintroduced uniforms of a more relaxed character. Many older people still wear traditional clothes called *hanbok*, while almost all Koreans will wear them for special occasions, such as New Year visiting.

Traditional dress has many forms. For men, it is usually a short jacket worn with full trousers tied at the ankles. These can be made of white cloth—the fashion for wearing white, associated with purity, was once so widespread among men and women that the Koreans were known as "the white-clad people". The stovepipe hats, called *satkat* and woven out of black horsehair and then varnished, are rare nowadays, although once they were worn by officials and for special occasions. The hats had to be high to contain the topknot: Korean men did not cut their hair, but wore it in a plait until marriage and in a topknot thereafter. Women's traditional outfit consists of a short blouse worn over a white shift and a long skirt, often made of brilliantly coloured brocade.

The two most important birthdays for a Korean are the first and the sixtieth. It used to be only a few people who survived until their sixtieth birthday, so it was an occasion for great rejoicing. Nowadays it is much more common, but still enthusiastically celebrated. Many children used to die in their first year of life due to the poor standard of living and medical care, but today many more survive.

On its first birthday, the child is dressed in traditional clothes and seated in front of a table covered with various objects. The first thing he or she takes is thought to symbolize the future. For example, thread means a long life; rice means plenty of food; a paint brush means scholarship; money means riches; and a bow or arrow means a military life.

Choosing a child's name is a very serious matter in South

Korea. Shamans and Confucian sages may be consulted to ensure that the right name, which will bring good fortune to its bearer, has been selected. Some parents simply call their children the Korean equivalent of "clever" or "beautiful", hoping that they will grow up to match their names.

Most Koreans have three names. The family name comes first, followed by the given name, which usually consists of two parts. One of these parts sometimes identifies the generation to which a person belongs, while the other is rather like names given in the West.

Some Koreans westernize their names, by putting the family name after the given names, as did the former president Syngman Rhee.

The ancient custom of using personal seals *(tojong)* on all documents reflects the importance of names in South Korea. Everybody has his or her own seal carved in jade, ivory, wood or other material, which is used instead of a signature.

Today, longer life and taller children are just two indicators that the health of Koreans has improved as their country has become richer. Most town houses and villages now have running water, so hygiene is improving. Nowadays, with more money and education, people are able to eat better as well. Nearly half the people have health insurance to help pay medical bills. But there is still a shortage of medical facilities in the countryside and for the poor in the towns, and diseases such as tuberculosis and intestinal worms are widespread.

Many Koreans favour Oriental medicine, which includes

An old man wearing *the hanbok*—the traditional costume consisting of a tall hat and a long jacket tied at the front and worn for religious occasions

acupuncture (the use of needles to stimulate various parts of the body), massage and heat stimulation. They also use a variety of herbs (including the famous ginseng) and other medicinal ingredients (such as the very popular powdered deer's antlers). People often use both Western and Oriental medicine and both can be studied at Korean universities.

Up until the end of the nineteenth century, schooling was

A ginseng stall offers the root in jars, or as tablets, powders or teabags to Koreans favouring Oriental medicine

very traditional and restricted, not only to the rich but also to boys. Then Christian missionaries arrived and introduced Western-style education, including schools for girls and the first universities.

Koreans put a very high value on education and children are expected to work extremely hard. Primary schooling is free and compulsory from the age of seven to thirteen, but anything after that has to be paid for by the child's family. Although the government planned to make all middle-school education free by 1985, this aim has not yet been achieved, and poorer parents have to rely on their savings, or scholarships and other forms of assistance. More than eighty per cent of children go on to the next three years of middle school. At the third stage, high school, it is not uncommon for the students to work from 6.30 in the morning until midnight, so great is their—and their parents'—determination to get into college.

Nearly one-third of those leaving secondary schools go on to one of Korea's hundred universities. There are also more than a hundred junior colleges for less academic studies. With such a large proportion of Korea's young people becoming college graduates, it is often difficult for them to find suitable jobs. More boys than girls go on to college and all young men have to spend up to three years in the armed forces, as military service is compulsory.

Very few girls pursue a career. Most stay at home when they get married and many employers insist on women leaving their jobs when they become mothers. The women in the family are in charge of the house, cooking and children and they are expected to obey men, allowing them to have the best food and to make the important decisions. Traditionally, a girl's husband was chosen by the parents in consultation with a professional matchmaker. Nowadays many young people choose their own partners, or the choice is made jointly by parents, matchmakers and children.

Weddings used to be so lavish that the government has introduced some restrictions. However, there are still large parties and generous presents. Although weddings used to take place in the bride's home, nowadays the most common place is a wedding hall, though temples and churches are also used. The ceremony is similar to the one in the West and may well be followed by a traditional Confucian-style ceremony. After marriage, a girl is usually considered to belong to her husband's family, but she does not change her name. The most powerful person in her life becomes her new mother-in-law, while her links with her own parents become more distant. Traditionally, until she has a son, she has not earned respect in her new family.

Each person appears on a family register (a girl usually being removed from her own and entering her husband's on marriage). The main copy of this official document is kept at the family's place of origin and it is the responsibility of the official head of the family. People on the same family register

A South Korean family. Once married, the woman usually stays at home to look after the children

cannot marry each other. It used to be important to have sons to ensure continuation of the family register, and although this is no longer as crucial, most people still prefer a son to a daughter.

Work conditions are exceptionally hard in Korea. Shops are usually open seven days a week and the average working week in the manufacturing industry, 54.4 hours, is one of the longest in the world. In offices, there is a five-and-a-half-day week and it is very common for junior staff to work from eight o'clock in the morning to seven o'clock in the evening, the principle being that they should arrive well before the senior members of staff and leave after them. In addition to this, the workers may have only a few days' annual holiday (as well as the public holidays). Conditions for working women tend to be even harder than for men.

Drinking is a popular pastime among Korean men, who have a reputation for enjoying large amounts of alcohol. There are a variety of drinking establishments. Cheap ones include small parlours for drinking beer, *makkoli* (a light rice wine), or *soju* (a spirit made from sweet potatoes), while the *kisaeng* houses—where the famous hostesses, called *kisaeng* in Korean, entertain the customers with music, dancing, games and witty conversation—require a well-filled wallet. All drinking places will serve some food, as Koreans consider it rude to serve alcohol without the accompanying food, called *anju*.

Other popular entertainments are cinema, theatre, concerts, dance performances and sports—spurred on by Korea's

Boys playing in a Kwangju street. Many South Koreans believe that sons are necessary for the continuation of the family register and therefore prefer them to daughters

outstanding performance in the 1986 Asian Games and the excellent facilities prepared for the 1988 Olympic Games. The Koreans are enormously hospitable and like to make friends, therefore parties and eating out consume large amounts of time and money.

Most Koreans do not have such expensive possessions as video recorders, freezers or cars. Even those with enough money to buy these prefer to save it to ensure that there is enough to pay for their children's or grandchildren's education (and university education can cost about forty per cent of an average family's income), or to pay for their health insurance and retirement. Koreans save nearly one-third of their earnings.

Towns and cities have good transport systems, including cheap trains, buses and taxis, as well as excellent underground services in Seoul and Pusan. Despite the scarcity of private cars, the roads are very crowded. At rush hours, the ten- and twelve-lane motorways into the main working areas of Seoul are packed with traffic, with one of the highest accident rates in the world.

Korea is the world's fourth most densely populated country, with 408 people per square kilometre, or about 1,000 per square mile. Since most of the population is concentrated in the cities, people have had to learn to cope with crowded conditions. Although Koreans find it acceptable for people to push past each other in crowded places, they expect everyone to queue fairly where appropriate. They appreciate good manners and respond with great courtesy. Their politeness, together with their great sense of fun, has helped them adapt to the problems of urban life.

The Countryside

Around 1900, more than two-thirds of the Korean people were farmers. However, most of them did not own the land they farmed—they were slaves, servants or tenants on the land of rich landowners. Less than one-fifth of Korea's land was cultivated and most of that gave a poor return for the farmer's hard work due to bad soil, mountainous terrain, a harsh climate and difficulties in getting goods to market.

During the Japanese occupation (1910-45), the land was carefully surveyed and ownership recorded. Many big farms had Japanese owners, who cleared extra land for farming as well as reclaiming some land from the sea. They introduced irrigation, which made more fields suitable for growing rice, Korea's main food and most important crop. They also began building good roads and railways, to help farmers take their produce to market.

After 1945, the United States Military Government transferred the land which had belonged to Japanese landowners to

A farmer walks home from his field. Better roads have helped South Korean farmers, who can now transport their produce to the town markets more quickly and easily

the Koreans who were working on it. In the 1949-50 period, the first Korean government tried to reduce all farms to less than 3 hectares (7.5 acres), selling the extra land to the tenant farmers. As a result, most farming in Korea has been on small family plots whose average size is about 0.9 hectare (2.25 acres).

During the 1960s, there was an enormous increase in industry and prosperity in South Korea. The earnings on the farms did not increase as much as those in the towns, so many people moved from the countryside to work in the cities. As a result, less than one-sixth of the population now farms. In

A village farmhouse, with the clothes line, water pump and dilapidated bicycle familiar in villages the world over. Corrugated roofs have replaced the traditional thatching

1971, President Park's government realized that something must be done to improve life for the farmers and launched the *Saemaul Undong* ("New Community Movement"). The aim of this movement was to encourage farmers to work hard to improve life for themselves. This included cooperation in community projects.

However, the government realized that if outside experts tried to introduce community projects and modern farming methods, the farmers would be unlikely to cooperate. They had to win their support first. Therefore, the first part of the *Saemaul Undong* involved improving life for individual families. The government made available cement and other materials and encouraged people to improve their homes—in particular their roofs, (which at that time were mostly thatched), their kitchens and their washing and toilet facilities, which were very simple and rather unhealthy.

Once popular support had been won for these projects, villages were encouraged to cooperate to improve their basic services, such as roads and drains. Again, materials and advice were provided, but this time villagers not only had to do the work: they also had to cooperate with the other members of the village to agree on the projects and work together. This involved choosing village leaders and holding meetings. The final and continuing stage, once people have shown that they are prepared to work hard to complete projects and to cooperate with other villagers, involves projects to earn money.

These farmers are working to build reinforced banks to a river, as part of a cooperative community project

These include common seedbeds, fish-farming, growing of vegetables in vinyl houses, joint transport and storage of farm produce and helping farmers borrow money to buy machinery. More than a quarter of South Korea's 1.2 million farmers now have a powered tiller. However, draught animals are still widely used. Korean cattle have been bred largely to help on the land and are famous for their strength and gentleness. Being working animals they are very tough to eat, so different cattle are bred for beef and milk.

The *Saemaul Undong* also helped introduce other modern methods of farming, such as growing high-yield strains of rice effectively. This involved improving the irrigation systems and using chemical fertilizers and pesticides. The amount grown

A farmer ploughing his field with a bull. Draught animals are still widely used to draw carts and ploughs—they are a lot cheaper than machines

Transplanting rice seedlings to a field. In preparation for this, the field, known as a rice paddy, has been flooded with water and thoroughly ploughed

has increased to such an extent that South Korea's rice yield of about 5 tonnes per hectare (2 tons per acre) is one of the highest in the world. Some disadvantages of this remarkable increase in fertility are that the manufacture of the pesticides and fertilizers uses large amounts of petrol which South Korea has to import at great expense. Also, the insects have become resistant to the pesticides, so more and more have to be used for the same effect. Some of the pesticides and fertilizers then pollute the water supplies. Farmers tend to spray more often than they should in the hope that this will have an even better effect; instead, it can cause poisoning.

The two most important crops have always been rice and

A fishing boat moored offshore near Cheju Island. Larger vessels from South Korea can be found in all parts of the world

barley, which still account for about a half of farmers' incomes. The barley is grown on hilly land and also in the south, on rice fields during the winter, after the rice has been harvested and before the new rice is planted in the spring. South Korea grows enough of these two grains for its needs.

However, people are now wanting to eat a wider variety of grains, more vegetables (in addition to the popular cabbage and white radish, essential for *kimchi*) and many more animal products (requiring grains for feed, as Korea is very short of grasslands for grazing). The main food imports are maize, wheat and soya beans, of which the USA is the chief supplier.

Fishing and forestry are important countryside activities. Like farming, these have been greatly modernized since 1970 thanks to the *Saemaul* movement. Korean fishing vessels, which used to go all over the world, have now been hampered by the fishing restrictions introduced by other countries. In an effort to overcome these problems, Korean fishing communities are being established overseas—in Argentina a settlement has been started which will include 122 Korean fishing families, a large trawler and a fish-processing plant.

In spite of decreasing numbers of people living in the countryside, the Koreans have strong country links. Not only do the most popular forms of music and dance come from the countryside, but people are very conscious of where the men in their family come from. At *Chusok*, the autumn festival when Koreans remember their ancestors, more than ten million people—about a quarter of the population—leave the towns and cities to renew their roots in the country.

Into the Twenty-first Century

Koreans who travel overseas joke that they can be away from London, Paris or New York for six years, but on return still recognize these cities and find their way around easily. In contrast, if they are away from Seoul for even six months, they are lost on their return. Certainly, some aspects of life in South Korea, such as buildings, roads and facilities, are changing incredibly fast, spurred on by the phenomenal economic growth. Life in the Republic of Korea is also becoming more and more different from that of its northern neighbour with whom it has had almost no contact since the 1950s.

Most South Koreans feel very sad about having no contact with North Koreans, especially as some of them have close relatives in the North. They would like both halves of the country to enter the United Nations and to become more friendly to each other.

The people of South Korea are extremely patriotic. They

are proud of their country's meteoric progress from being a poor, uneducated nation to one that can compete on the international stage. Their patriotism comes mainly from their traditional distrust of outsiders. For many centuries, they have had to resist foreign invasions. Even now, they have the sixth largest army in the world (North Korea's) stationed on their border; and, in 1983, four of their ministers, together with thirteen other South Koreans, were killed by an allegedly North Korean bomb while on an overseas visit to Rangoon in Burma. Besides this distrust, very few South Koreans are allowed to travel overseas and get to know other cultures for themselves: they cannot obtain passports for tourist travel until they are over fifty-five. Business and educational travel are also controlled.

However, their links with other countries have had to become closer. Their security is dependent on the United Nations forces, the vast majority of which are the forty thousand US troops stationed in South Korea. Thousands of Koreans marry Americans each year and many more go to the United States as students or immigrants. There are also large Korean communities in China (1.2 million), Japan (600,000), the USA (500,000) and the USSR.

In addition, trade forces the Koreans to get to know and understand other cultures. Again, the USA is the most important, being the chief importer of South Korea's exports. As a result, the Koreans have had to accept some of the customs of international business. Such acceptance is not

Seoul riot police ready to confront the demonstrators in 1987, the year in which protests and riots against government abuses spread to all sections of the population

always popular, and is one of the causes of the continual public protests.

Many South Koreans have strong feelings about how the nation should choose its president, preferring a direct election system to the electoral college system of the Fifth Republic. They also worry about the gap between the rich and the poor, which is now growing. In nineteenth-century Korea, there were major class differences. These were reduced dramatically, first by the Japanese colonization and then by the devastation of the Korean War. Most Koreans are anxious that the wealth of the country should now be fairly shared, and that everyone should have adequate accommodation and health care, as well as freedom of speech and justice under the law.

If all this can be achieved while the country continues its remarkable economic growth, South Korea will be ready to enter the twenty-first century having attained its official national goals of peace, unity and prosperity.

Index

Ahn Chung-gun 32
alphabet *(hangul)* 28-29, 59
Altaic people 20
animals *see* fauna
anju 79
archery 61
Asian Games 62

bamboo 12, 64
barley *see* crops
birds 15-16
birthdays, special 73
bodhisattva 53
Buddha's Birthday 60
Buddhism 52-54
bulgogi 71-72
business leaders 47

calendar (lunar) 58
cattle 86
celadons 66, 67
chaebol 44
Cheju Island 9, 12
Children's Day 59
China, links with 21, 22, 23, 25, 26, 30, 35-36, 40, 91
Chondogyo 56-57
Choson
    meaning 9-10
        Ancient Choson 19-20
        Choson dynasty 26
        North Korea 36
Christianity 54-55, 57
Chun Doo Hwan 37
Chusok 59, 89
climate 8-9
Confucianism 26, 50-52, 57
constitutions 37, 38
crops
    barley 88
    rice 82, 86, 88

dance 49, 62-63, 80
Demilitarized Zone (DMZ) 16, 35

Democratic People's Republic of Korea (North Korea) 8, 33, 34, 35, 36, 90, 91
dress
    traditional 72-73
    modern 72

education 75-77, 81
electoral system 37
electronic industry 42, 44
entertainment 61-63, 79-80

family life 69, 77-78, 89
family register 78
farming 85-88
fauna 15-17
Feast of the Lanterns *see* Buddha's Birthday
festivals 19, 58-60, 89
fishing 88-89
five-year plans 41
flora 12-14, 16
food 17, 71-72, 79, 88
forests 14
Foundation Day 19
foundation myth 18-19
furniture 69-70

geography 9-10
gingko trees 12-13
ginseng 13, 75
government 33, 37-38

Halla, Mount 9
Han River 47
hanbok see dress, traditional
Hanguk 36-37
hangul see alphabet
health care 74-75
Hermit Kingdom 29-30
housing 68-70, 85
hwabaek 21
hwarang 23

Inchon 11, 68
Inchon landing 34
industry 32, 40-45
irrigation 82, 86
Islam 57
islands 9

Japan, links with 26, 29, 31-33, 39, 40, 91

Kaegyong (ancient Kaesong) 25
kalbi 71-72
Kim Il Sung 33, 35
kimchi 71, 88
kisaeng houses 79
Koguryo 22
Kojong, King 31, 32
Kongju 22
Korea, origin of the name 25
Korean art 64-67
Korean Independence Army 32
Korean War
 history 33-36
 economic consequences 40
Koryo 25-26
kut 48, 55
Kwangju rebellion 37
Kyongju 23-24

land reform 82-83

MacArthur, Douglas 34, 35
Mahayana Buddhism 53-54
makkoli 79
Manchurian crane *see* birds
marriage 77-78
medicine 75
Military Armistice Commission (MAC) 35-36
Mongol invasions 25-26
mountains 9-10
mudang, 48-49, 57
music 62-63

names 74
National Council for Democratic Constitution 37

national debt 44-45
New Community Movement *see Semaul Undong*
North Korea *see* Democratic People's Republic of Korea

Olympic Games (1988) 38, 62

Paekche 22
Paleoasians 20
Panmunjom 36
Paris Peace Conference 33
Park Chung Hee 37
population 8, 68
Pusan 46, 62, 68
Puyo 22
Pyongyang 19

Rangoon bombing 91
reforestation 14
religions 48-57
Rhee, Syngman 33, 37, 74
rice *see* crops
roads 32, 41, 46, 82
Roh Tae Woo 37
rose of Sharon 12

sam taeguk 52
Samil movement 33
schools 75-77
Semaul Undong 84-86, 89
Sejong, King 27-28
Seoul 9, 11, 33, 38, 46, 68, 81, 90
shamanism 48-49, 54
shipbuilding 40
Silla
 history 23-24
 jewellery 66-67
snakes 17
soju 79
sports 61-62
ssirum 61
Sunjong, King 31

Taegu 1, 62, 68
Taegukki 64
taekwondo 61

Taejon 62
Tangun 19, 20, 56
Taoism 52, 64-65
tidal range 10-11
tigers 18
tojong 74
towns 9, 11, 62, 68
transport 81
Tristram woodpecker *see* birds
Tsushima Island 27
turtle ships 29

Ullung Island 12
unemployment 39, 77
Union of Soviet Socialist Republics, links with 33, 91
United Nations Organization, links with 33, 34, 45, 36
United States of America, links with 29, 30, 33-35, 45, 83, 91
universities 77

women's roles 77-78
Wang Kon 23-24
wildlife *see* fauna

Yi dynasty 26
Yi Song-gye 26
Yi Sun-shin 29
yo 69
yudo 61

Zen Buddhism 54